blasta (blastə) *adj* From the Irish language, meaning delicious, tasty, appetising. Rhymes with pasta.

Blasta Books are to cookbooks what street food is to restaurants: a fun, accessible and affordable way to eat exciting food.

At Blasta Books, we believe that the two things that connect everyone, everywhere, are food and stories. If you draw a Venn diagram with **food** in one circle and **stories** in the other, **connection** is what's in the middle where the circles overlap. Food and stories are what we all have in common, no matter who we are or where we're from.

That's why we're working to make more room at the table, one bite and one book at a time. Pull up a chair and dig in.

beans

Recipes for a Pulse-Powered Future

by Ali Honour

contents

Introduction 1
Bean basics 4

snacks & sides

Sprouted beans 8
Hummus loaded with roast veggies 10
Red lentil and flaxseed bread with seed butter 12
Fermented fava bean wraps 13
Crispy salt and pepper pods 14
Harissa chickpea balls with pickled aubergine,
feta and lemon yogurt 16
Kidney bean and beetroot falafel 18
Spiced dal fritters 19
Chilli beans with crispy smashed spuds 20
Burrata with chilli, garlic, lentil and caper oil 22
Confit butter beans with garlic, rosemary and thyme 23

salads, soups & stews

Green bean salad with red onion and aubergine pickle 24
Pulse-powered changemakers 26
Roast beetroot salad with minty peas, pickled stems,
beet leaves and ricotta 28
Pea and broad bean broth with noodles 30
Roast tomato gazpacho with crispy beans and pesto 32
Beany, shroomy stew with dumplings 34

mains

Lentil, walnut and mushroom rissoles 36
Five ways with beans 40
Clearing the air: The truth about toots 41
Crispy pea risotto cakes with mint dressing and aquafaba mayo .. 42
The Bean Queen burger 44

on the side

What in the world is aquafaba? 46
Aquafaba mayo 47
Black-eyed bean ketchup 49
Chocolate bean spread 51

sweet

Berry bean muffins 52
Chocolate chip, ginger and white bean crinkle cookies 53
Dreamy beany doughnuts 54
Sticky toffee bean and parsnip pudding 56
White bean crème brûlée 58
Black bean baked Alaska 60
Black bean mocha fudge cake 62

drinks

Podka 64
The faba-lush cocktail 66

introduction

I'm a chef and food systems agitator who wholeheartedly believes that how we eat can help fix our broken world.

My journey with beans started as a chef looking for ways to feed people well without wrecking the planet. The more I worked with beans, the more they revealed themselves as reliable, sustainable and full of possibility. They became more than an ingredient – they became the backbone of a better way to eat.

Beans don't usually get top billing. They hide in the back of the pantry, waiting to bulk out a stew or play sidekick to something more glamorous. But it's time for that to change. Beans are having a moment, and frankly, it's long overdue.

beans for balance

Our food system is broken. We're burning through land, water and energy at a rate that is unsustainable. We're producing food that often does more harm than good, even while millions of people don't have enough of it. At the same time, supermarkets are stacked with ultra-processed products pretending to be dinner. There's no single silver-bullet solution to all these problems, but beans come pretty close.

These small but mighty ingredients tick every box that matters. Beans are nutrient-dense, affordable, climate-friendly and can be grown in a way that improves the soil rather than exhausts it. Beans give more than they take, and that's rare.

But beans are also criminally underrated in the kitchen. They're not just good for you, they're good full stop. They can be creamy, crunchy, smoky, spicy, sweet, savoury and satisfying. And in the right hands, they're anything but boring.

This book puts beans centre stage. Not in a worthy, preachy way, but because they deserve it. They're delicious, adaptable and wildly underappreciated. Whether you're a seasoned legume lover or just bean curious, these recipes will surprise you, without a sad three-bean salad in sight. Instead, you'll find dishes that are bold, bright and packed with unexpected flavours. These are beans with big ambitions.

This book also has a low-waste, root-to-tip ethos running through it. I want you to use the skins, stems and scraps and turn them into something delicious, because cooking with care, cooking creatively and cooking sustainably are all one and the same.

the future is delicious

Growing up in Oxford in the UK, some of my earliest memories are of picking peas and beans in my grandparents' garden, popping open the pods and eating them before they even made it to the kitchen. That early connection to food – the joy of growing it, harvesting it and savouring it fresh – stayed with me. That same sense of wonder and respect for the earth continues to drive everything I do today.

Throughout my 30-year career in kitchens and the food industry, zero-waste practices, seasonal, plant-focused dishes and responsible sourcing have always been priorities. More recently, I have dived into the broader world of food systems, working on regenerative farms, in community food projects and at global summits, all fuelled by one simple belief: we need to change the way we eat.

If we're going to eat less meat (and we really should), then we need plant-based dishes that don't feel like a downgrade. Beans have texture, body and real depth of flavour. They carry spices beautifully. They work across cultures and cuisines. And they fill you up without emptying your wallet or draining the planet's resources.

Every recipe in this book is vegetarian, not because meat is the enemy, but because I want to show how beans can carry the whole plate. When we eat more plants, especially protein-rich ones like beans, we lighten the load on the planet. But more importantly, we eat well.

These dishes aren't about sacrifice, they're about satisfaction, flavour and texture. Beans fill you up, fuel your body and taste like something you want to eat, not something you're being told you should. Beans aren't just a pantry staple – they're the future. And as you'll see for yourself in these recipes, the future is delicious.

beans for life

Every project I take on is rooted in the idea that food should be delicious, nutritious, accessible and resilient for us, for the planet and for future generations.

I've worked on everything from supporting the shift to plant-based protein options in mainstream diets to designing zero-waste menus for events and pop-ups and running circular-system-conscious catering events for the Blue Earth Summit, where we celebrated food that doesn't just taste great, but feeds into a larger narrative of sustainability and waste reduction.

I'm deeply involved with initiatives like Beans Is How, where we champion beans as a crucial ingredient in a more sustainable, healthy and resilient food system. Beans are the unsung heroes of the plant-based world. They're climate-resilient, nutritious and versatile. They require fewer resources than animal agriculture and can regenerate the soil, making them an essential part of the solution to the climate crisis.

As a member of the Chefs' Manifesto, I also work with chefs around the world to promote the UN Sustainable Development Goals and advocate for sustainable, plant-forward food systems. I focus on making sustainable food choices not just accessible, but exciting, flavourful and easy to incorporate into everyday life.

For me, food has always been a way to connect, educate and inspire change. With this book, I hope to show that with beans, we can make a difference to our health, our communities and the planet. It's my contribution to a larger movement towards a healthier, more sustainable food system. Every bean dish you cook is a small, silent protest against a broken food system. A delicious, nutritious rebellion. A fart in the face of industrial agriculture.

Here's to full bellies, healthy guts and a planet that might just survive past the dinner table.

bean basics

Whether you're pulling a tin off the shelf for a lightning-fast dinner or soaking dried beans overnight, you're already winning. There's no rivalry here, just options.

Tinned beans are quick and convenient, but cooking with dried beans is easy, rewarding and surprisingly therapeutic. It's about slowing down, building flavour and turning something simple into something delicious. Dried beans are also more economical, more versatile and give you complete control over seasoning and texture.

Why try dried?

❶ FLAVOUR AND TEXTURE: You get to infuse your beans with aromatics, salt them to your taste and cook them to that perfect creamy stage.

❷ VALUE FOR MONEY: Dried beans triple in size when cooked. That means a 500g (1lb 2oz) bag of dried beans is like Mary Poppins's handbag: it goes a surprisingly long way.

❸ SUSTAINABLE AND LOW WASTE: Dried beans need minimal packaging and no brine. Plus they store well and are easy to batch-cook and freeze.

❹ KITCHEN EMPOWERMENT: There's something deeply satisfying about transforming a dry, rock-hard nugget into a plump, buttery beauty. It feels like magic.

soaking

Soaking beans means better **flavour**, better **texture** and better **digestion**. Soaking also reduces the cooking time. So let's demystify the process. There's no witchcraft or special equipment, just water, salt and time.

❶ OVERNIGHT SOAK: THE GOLD STANDARD Measure your beans – let's say 100g (½ cup) dried beans (one tin's worth for reference). Rinse the beans to remove any dust or rebel pebbles, then put them in a large bowl and cover with plenty of cold water (at least three times their volume, as they'll swell). Soak for 8–12 hours or overnight, then drain and rinse before cooking.

❷ QUICK SOAK: FOR THE FORGETFUL OR IMPATIENT Rinse the beans, then pop them in a large pot with at least three times their volume of water. Boil for 5 minutes, then turn off the heat, cover the pot with a lid and let them sit for 1 hour. Drain and rinse. It's not quite as flavourful as the overnight method, but it works.

How much dried beans equal a tin?

Here's the bean maths made simple:

1 x 400g (14oz) tin of beans = 100–125g (½ cup) dried beans = 250–300g (1½ cups) cooked beans

So if a recipe calls for one tin of beans, you can use 100–125g (½ cup) dried beans, soak them, then cook them. But if you're going to the trouble of soaking and cooking beans, I recommend doing at least 250g (1½ cups) dried beans to get roughly 2½–3 tins' worth. Pop the extras in the fridge or freezer (see below).

---

storing

If you've soaked and cooked more beans than you need for a single recipe, you can **store** extra beans in an airtight container in the fridge for up to five days. Or to **freeze** the extras, just portion them into containers with a little of the cooking liquid. Make sure you **label** them with the type of bean they are and the date, otherwise you won't remember which beans are which.

cook gently, cook well

Think of it less like boiling and more like a gentle bean spa.

Pop your soaked, drained beans into a pot. Cover with enough fresh cold water to cover the beans by 5cm (2in). Now add your aromatics, such as one bay leaf and/or a few sprigs of fresh thyme; one small, unpeeled, halved onion; one celery stalk; two unpeeled, smashed garlic cloves; and one whole fresh chilli for a bit of kick. Bring to a boil, then skim off any foamy scum that floats to the top – it's not harmful, but it's not pleasing to the eye either. Reduce the heat to the gentlest possible simmer. Cover the pot partially with a lid and cook just until the beans are tender (see the cooking times on the next page). Now add 1 teaspoon of salt, then check the beans every 20–30 minutes. Soaked beans won't turn to mush unless you boil the life out of them (the salt helps to prevent this), but one of the advantages of cooking dried beans is being able to cook them to the perfect texture. Taste the beans halfway through the cooking time and add more salt if needed. But have you ever cooked beans and found that they just never got to that perfect texture? When that happens, it might be because the beans were old or weren't soaked for long enough. If you know you're working with old beans, give them the gold standard soak and add 1 teaspoon baking soda or a bit of kombu to the cooking water to help break them down.

❶ **HOW TO COOK BEANS IN A PRESSURE COOKER:** Cooking beans in a pressure cooker is a game-changer – quick, efficient and perfect for batch prep. Start by rinsing your dried beans and checking for any small stones or debris. Soaking is optional, but if you soak them for 6–8 hours (or overnight), they'll cook even faster and be easier to digest. Add the same aromatics as above along with 1 teaspoon baking soda or a piece of kombu seaweed to boost the cooking. Lock the lid and cook for the time outlined on page 7. Let the pressure release naturally for the best texture. Drain or keep that liquid gold (see below). That's it! Tender, plain beans, ready for anything.

❷ **DON'T DITCH THE LIQUID GOLD!** That leftover cooking water, often called pot liquor, is bean broth at its finest. Don't chuck it! Use it in soups, stews, risottos and grain dishes, or freeze it in an ice cube tray to add to a stock later. For any white bean liquor, once reduced, you have aquafaba (see page 46).

a guide to cooking times

TYPE OF BEAN	COOKING TIME (AFTER SOAKING)	COOKING TIME IN A PRESSURE COOKER (UNSOAKED)	COOKING TIME IN A PRESSURE COOKER (AFTER SOAKING)
black beans	45–60 MINUTES	25–30 MINUTES	10–12 MINUTES
black-eyed beans	45–60 MINUTES	25–30 MINUTES	10–15 MINUTES
borlotti beans	45–60 MINUTES	30–35 MINUTES	15–20 MINUTES
butter beans	50–70 MINUTES	30–35 MINUTES	14–18 MINUTES
cannellini beans	60–75 MINUTES	20–25 MINUTES	12–15 MINUTES
Carlin peas	45–50 MINUTES	20–30 MINUTES	15–18 MINUTES
chickpeas	60–90 MINUTES	35–40 MINUTES	15–18 MINUTES
fava beans	DON'T NEED SOAKING*	20–25 MINUTES	10–12 MINUTES
haricot beans	35–40 MINUTES	20–25 MINUTES	12–15 MINUTES
kidney beans	60–75 MINUTES	30–35 MINUTES	12–15 MINUTES
lentils	DON'T NEED SOAKING*	20–25 MINUTES	10–15 MINUTES

*Unless using in breads, pancakes or fritters

Sprouted beans are a great way to add nutrients to your diet and are easy to digest, so they're a good place to start your bean journey. Once you start sprouting your own beans, you'll be hooked. You can sprout so many kinds of beans, like mung, aduki, chickpeas, peas and kidney beans, as well as lentils (green, brown or black work best). Throw them on top of just about anything.

sprouted beans

MAKES 1 LARGE JAR

200g (1 cup) dried beans (see the intro)

750ml (3 cups) water, for soaking

Put the beans in a fine mesh sieve and rinse them under cold running water. Put them in a large jar, then cover with the 750ml (3 cups) water, seal the jar with a lid and let them soak for 8–12 hours at room temperature.

Drain the beans in a fine mesh sieve and rinse them well under cold water. Put them back in the jar, ensuring they are damp but that there's no excess water.

how to use sprouted beans

- Add to salads, wraps and sandwiches
- Blend into dips or hummus
- Stir into soups or curries
- Lightly sauté for a warm side dish

Seal the jar with a lid and store in a cool, dark place, such as a cupboard, tilted at an angle for proper drainage. Rinse and drain the beans every 8–12 hours (twice daily). After 24–48 hours, small sprouts will start to appear.

Continue this rinsing and draining process for up to three days, depending on how long you want your sprouts to grow.

Once the beans have sprouted to your desired length (2.5cm (1in) is ideal), give them a final rinse, then store them in an airtight container in the fridge for up to five days.

hummus loaded with roast veggies

SERVES 4

Turn a tin of chickpeas and a few veggies into a meal or sharing plate. A classic hummus is easy to make and costs pennies compared to the shop-bought versions. You can use whatever veggies you have or what's in season. When I wrote this recipe, I had onions, carrots, squash and garlic.

250g (1½ cups) cooked chickpeas or 1 x 400g (14oz) tin, drained and rinsed (save the aquafaba for the mayo on page 47)

1 garlic clove

zest and juice of ½ lemon

60ml (¼ cup) rapeseed oil

2–3 tbsp tahini

a little water

FOR THE ROAST VEGGIES:

400g (14oz) squash, peeled, deseeded and cut into chunks (keep the seeds and toast them for a snack)

3 medium carrots, cut lengthways or into chunks

2 medium onions, cut into wedges

4 garlic cloves, left whole and unpeeled

2 tbsp rapeseed oil

1 tsp ground cumin (optional)

1 tsp ground coriander (optional)

a few sprigs of fresh thyme or rosemary (optional)

1 tsp sea salt

½ tsp ground black pepper

100g (3½oz) kale, torn into bite-sized pieces (optional)

2 tsp white and/or black sesame seeds (optional)

a pinch of chilli flakes (optional)

TO SERVE:

your best extra-virgin olive oil

a handful of fresh herbs, such as parsley or coriander

zest and juice of ½ lemon

Preheat the oven to 180°C (350°F).

Put the squash, carrots, onions and garlic on a large baking tray. Drizzle with the rapeseed oil, then season with the spices and herbs (if using) and the salt and pepper. Toss to coat the veg in the oil and seasoning, then spread them out in a single layer.

Roast in the preheated oven for 30–40 minutes, stirring halfway through for even cooking. Remove the tray from the oven and scatter the kale over the roasted veg (if using), then return the tray to the oven and cook for another 5–7 minutes, until the kale is crispy.

Meanwhile, to make the hummus, put the chickpeas in a food processor with the garlic, lemon zest and juice, oil and tahini, then blitz for a minute. Add 1 teaspoon of water at a time until you get a smooth, creamy consistency. Season with salt to taste, then set aside or refrigerate until needed.

When the veg are done, squeeze the roasted garlic out of its skins, then mix it through the vegetables along with the sesame seeds and a pinch of chilli flakes (if using).

To serve, spread the hummus on a serving platter. Top with the roasted veggies, then drizzle with a good extra-virgin olive oil and sprinkle over the chopped fresh herbs and the lemon zest and juice.

variation

To make a beetroot hummus, see the tip on page 29.

This simple, nourishing loaf with an omega-3 boost from the flaxseeds is perfect for serving with soup or anything saucy. You can add any topping or filling you like. It's also a gluten-free alternative to traditional bread and it keeps soft for days. The seed butter is a great dairy-free alternative for a light, nutritious snack. All in all, these are two handy little recipes to have in your repertoire.

red lentil & flaxseed bread
with seed butter

MAKES 1 LOAF

200g (1 cup) dried red lentils

80ml (⅓ cup) water

35g (¼ cup) ground flaxseeds

1 tsp baking powder

¼ tsp baking soda

½ tsp salt

1 tbsp apple cider vinegar

a handful of seeds for the top (optional)

FOR THE SEED BUTTER:

250g (1½ heaped cups) mixed seeds or just your favourite seed

2–3 tbsp oil (I use rapeseed)

a pinch of salt

Put the lentils in a bowl, cover them with cold water and soak for 2 hours.

Preheat the oven to 180°C (350°F). Line a 900g (2lb) loaf tin with non-stick baking paper.

To make the seed butter, scatter the seeds onto a baking tray, then toast them in the preheated oven for 15 minutes. Allow to cool, then put the seeds in a food processor and blend until they've broken down into a flour-like texture.

With the motor still running, add the oil 1 tablespoon at a time and blend until you have a smooth paste. Add salt to taste, then transfer to a clean jar and store at room temperature (this makes approx. 300g (1⅓ cups) of seed butter).

To make the bread, drain the soaked lentils in a fine mesh sieve, then rinse them under cold running water. Put them in a blender or food processor with the 80ml (⅓ cup) water and blitz until smooth.

Put the ground flaxseeds, baking powder, baking soda and salt in a large bowl. Stir in the blitzed lentils and the vinegar, then let it sit for 10 minutes to thicken.

Pour the mixture into the lined tin. Level the top, then sprinkle with a handful of seeds (if using). Bake in the oven for 30–40 minutes, until the bread is firm and slightly golden.

Allow to cool in the tin on a wire rack before slicing and spreading with the seed butter.

Store-bought wraps? Flimsy, tasteless and not worth the money. These, on the other hand, are something else entirely. Made with fermented fava beans, they've got depth, they've got tang and they've got a subtle, nutty complexity that no supermarket wrap could ever dream of. Plus these are packed with all the gut-friendly goodness that comes with fermentation, so you can feel smug while you stuff your face. Soft yet sturdy, they're the perfect vehicle for whatever fillings you fancy. But if you're looking for inspiration, try them loaded with roasted veggies (see page 11), tangy pickles, a cooling hit of yogurt and a punchy chutney to bring it all together. Messy? Absolutely. Worth it? Every single bite.

fermented fava bean wraps

MAKES 4–6

150g (1 cup) dried fava beans (or mung beans or lentils)

240ml (1 cup) water

½ tsp salt

Put the beans in a bowl, cover them with plenty of cold water and soak overnight.

Drain the beans in a fine mesh sieve, then rinse them under cold running water. Put them in a blender with 120ml (½ cup) of the fresh water and the salt, then blend until smooth. Add the rest of the water and blend again until you have a smooth batter.

Pour the mixture into a clean bowl and cover it with a clean cloth. Let it ferment for one to two days in a warm place, until you notice a slightly sour aroma.

Heat up a large non-stick frying pan on a medium heat. If it's a proper non-stick pan, you don't need to add any oil. Pour a thin layer of the fermented batter onto the hot, dry pan, tilting the pan until the batter covers the base in an even layer. Cook on each side for 2 minutes, until golden and slightly crisp. Slide the wrap out of the pan, then repeat with the remaining batter. Fill your wraps with whatever you fancy.

Don't bin the pod! Fry those little green jackets in a light-as-air tempura batter, then drown them in a sticky chilli and garlic sauce. Finish with a zippy squeeze of lime, and boom – you've got sweet, salty, sour, crunchy bliss in one bite. A cold beer or a crisp white wine goes down a treat with these too.

crispy salt & pepper pods

SERVES 2 AS A STARTER OR SNACK

200g (7oz) fresh bean pods
60g (½ cup) plain flour
60g (½ cup) cornflour
½ tsp ground cumin
1 tsp salt
½ tsp ground black pepper
2 tbsp cold water (still or sparkling)
vegetable oil, for deep-frying

FOR THE SAUCE:
1 tbsp vegetable oil
2 garlic cloves, finely chopped
1–2 small fresh red chillies, finely chopped
1 tbsp gochujang
1 tbsp white wine vinegar
1 tbsp honey
2 tsp black sesame seeds

TO GARNISH:
fresh coriander or parsley leaves (optional)

TO SERVE:
lime wedges

Rinse the bean pods thoroughly, then pat them dry with a clean tea towel.

Put the plain flour, cornflour, cumin, salt and pepper in a shallow dish and mix to combine. Whisk in just enough cold water to make a loose batter.

Heat the vegetable oil in a deep-fryer to 180°C (350°F). If you don't have a deep-fryer, fill a high-sided saucepan with just enough oil to submerge the bean pods, but make sure the pan is no more than halfway full. Put the pan on a medium-high heat.

Dip each pod in the batter, ensuring it's evenly coated. Shake off any excess batter, then add the pods to the hot oil in batches – don't overcrowd the fryer or pan. Fry for 2–3 minutes, until the pods are golden brown and crispy. Be careful, as they may pop and sizzle in the hot oil.

Drain the fried pods on a plate lined with kitchen paper to absorb any excess oil. Sprinkle with a pinch of salt while they're still hot, then transfer to a serving dish.

To make the sauce, heat the oil in a small saucepan on a medium heat. Add the garlic and chillies and cook for about 1 minute, until crispy. Add the gochujang, vinegar, honey, sesame seeds and a pinch of salt. Bring to a simmer and cook for 1 minute, then remove the pan from the heat.

To serve, spoon the sauce over the pods. Garnish with fresh coriander or parsley and serve with lime wedges for squeezing over for extra zing.

This dish packs a punch with the creamy-spicy-pickle combo. It's a great one for entertaining too, as everything can be prepared ahead of time. In fact, the aubergine pickle is even better the next day. Keep a jar in the fridge to pep up salads, mezze platters or cheese and charcuterie boards.

harissa chickpea balls
with pickled aubergine, feta & lemon yogurt
MAKES 16–18

250g (1½ cups) cooked chickpeas or 1 x 400g (14oz) tin, drained and rinsed

1 small red onion, finely chopped

2 garlic cloves, finely chopped

2 tbsp chopped fresh coriander stalks (keep the leaves for garnish)

1 tbsp harissa

2 tsp ground cumin

1 tsp ground coriander

½ tsp smoked paprika

sea salt and freshly ground black pepper

2–3 tbsp fresh or dried breadcrumbs

olive oil, for frying

Harissa chickpea balls

Spiced dal fritters

FOR THE PICKLED AUBERGINE:

2–3 garlic cloves, thinly sliced

1 small fresh red chilli, thinly sliced (optional and not too hot or it will overpower the pickle)

160ml (²/₃ cup) water

100ml (⅓ cup + 4 tsp) apple cider vinegar

4 tbsp golden caster sugar or light brown sugar

1 tsp salt

1 tsp black peppercorns

1 small aubergine, cut lengthways, then thinly sliced into half moons

FOR THE LEMON YOGURT:

250g (1 cup) Greek yogurt

zest of 1 lemon

TO FINISH:

100g (3½oz) feta cheese

chopped fresh coriander leaves

Put the chickpeas, red onion, garlic, coriander stalks, harissa and spices in a food processor. Pulse until the mixture comes together but still has some texture. You may need to scrape down the sides of the processor and blend again.

Season with salt and pepper to taste. Add more harissa if you want the balls to be spicier. Transfer to a mixing bowl and add just enough breadcrumbs to bind it all together.

Form the mixture into small balls about the size of a walnut (you should get 16–18 balls). Put them on a baking tray and chill in the fridge for 20–30 minutes.

Meanwhile, to make the pickled aubergine, put everything except the aubergine in a saucepan. Bring to a boil, stirring to dissolve the sugar and salt. Reduce the heat and add the sliced aubergine. Simmer for 2–3 minutes, just until the aubergine slices start to soften but still have a slight crunch. Remove the pan from the heat and allow to cool.

Mix the yogurt and lemon zest together in a small bowl, then season to taste with salt and pepper.

Preheat the oven to 180°C (350°F).

Heat some olive oil in a large frying pan on a medium-high heat. Add the chickpea balls and cook until they are golden brown and crispy on all sides, turning them as needed. This should take 3–5 minutes in total. Put them back on the baking tray, then pop into the preheated oven for 8 minutes to heat through. (You could sear them in the pan ahead of time, then cook them through later.)

To serve, spoon the lemon yogurt onto a serving platter and spread it out. Put the chickpea balls on top, then put pickled aubergine slices in between the bean balls. Crumble the feta cheese over the dish, then sprinkle with chopped fresh coriander.

Kidney bean and beetroot falafel

These little ruby-red gems combine the earthy sweetness of beetroot with the hearty texture of red kidney beans, creating a colourful, nutrient-packed twist on a classic. They're perfect for stuffing into wraps, serving with salads or dipping into a tangy lemon yogurt (see page 17) with pickles on the side.

kidney bean & beetroot falafel

MAKES 12

250g (1½ cups) cooked kidney beans or 1 x 400g (14oz) tin, drained and rinsed

125g (½ cup) grated raw beetroot

1 small red onion, finely chopped

2 garlic cloves, finely chopped

1 tbsp tahini

1 tbsp lemon juice

30g (¼ cup) chickpea flour or plain flour

½ tsp baking powder

1 tbsp chopped fresh parsley or coriander (optional)

1 tsp ground cumin

1 tsp ground coriander

½ tsp smoked paprika

½ tsp salt

¼ tsp ground black pepper

1–2 tbsp olive oil

If you want to bake the falafel rather than fry them, preheat the oven to 180°C (350°F) and line a baking tray with non-stick baking paper.

Put the beans, beetroot, onion, garlic, tahini and lemon juice in a food processor and blend until combined but still slightly chunky.

Add the flour, baking powder, fresh herbs (if using), spices, salt and pepper. Pulse until it forms a thick mixture that holds together. If it's too wet, add a little more flour.

Shape into 12 small balls (about 30g (1oz) each).

If you're baking the falafel, put them on the lined baking tray and brush the tops with olive oil. Bake in the preheated oven for 20–25 minutes, turning them over halfway through, until cooked through.

To pan-fry the falafel, heat the oil in a large non-stick frying pan on a medium heat. Add the falafel and cook for 3–4 minutes on each side, until crispy and cooked through.

Serve warm.

Mung dal is getting a glow-up – soaked, spiced and blended with veggies, then fried until crispy and golden into morsels of joy. You can use mung beans or red lentils here, but the mung dal have a nutty depth that makes them my go-to for this recipe. The right accompaniments take these street food bites to the next level, so I go with a cooling, herby raita and a spicy chutney. Don't even bother pretending you'll stop at one.

spiced dal fritters

MAKES 12

170g (1 cup) dried mung dal, mung beans or red lentils

60ml (¼ cup) fresh cold water

4 spring onions, finely chopped

2 medium carrots, grated

1 small fresh green chilli, deseeded and finely chopped (optional)

1 small bunch of fresh coriander, stalks and leaves finely chopped

2 tsp nigella seeds

1 tsp garam masala

1 tsp ground coriander

1 tsp salt

1 tsp baking powder

1 egg

2 tbsp vegetable oil

TO SERVE:

raita or Greek yogurt

chutney

Put the mung dal, mung beans or lentils in a bowl, cover them with plenty of cold water and soak for 2 hours.

Drain, then put in a food processor with the fresh cold water and blitz to a rough paste, adding a little more water if needed to get the beans to blend.

Put the spring onions, carrots, chilli (if using), fresh coriander, spices, salt and baking powder in a large bowl and stir to combine. Add the bean paste and crack in the egg. Stir until it all comes together into a thick batter, adding a little more water if necessary.

Heat the oil in a large non-stick frying pan on a medium heat. Add 2–3 tablespoons of batter per fritter to the pan and spread it out a little. Don't cook too many at once so you don't overcrowd the pan. Cook for about 3 minutes, until small bubbles start to form on top of each fritter. Turn them over and cook the other side for 2–3 minutes, until golden.

Serve with a cooling raita or Greek yogurt and your favourite chutney.

make it a meal
Serve with a poached egg.

This is the culinary equivalent of an old married couple who still flirt outrageously at dinner parties. Like beans on toast but with ambitions, this is comfort food that's had a word with itself, bulked up with smoky chilli and planted on a throne of crispy-edged, smashed potatoes. It's cheap. It's filling. It's deeply gratifying. And if you don't end up scraping the plate like it owes you money, I can't help you. It goes without saying that these beans are obviously amazing on toast too.

chilli beans *with crispy smashed spuds*

SERVES 2 AS A STARTER OR SIDE

1 tbsp olive oil

1 small onion, finely chopped

2 garlic cloves, finely chopped

1 chipotle chilli in adobo, finely chopped, 1 tsp ancho chilli flakes or a few shakes of chipotle Tabasco

½ fresh red chilli, finely chopped (optional)

1 tsp ground cumin

1 tsp ground coriander

1 tsp smoked paprika

250g (1½ cups) cooked beans or 1 x 400g (14oz) tin, drained and rinsed (I use black beans or Carlin peas here, but any bean will work)

240ml (1 cup) passata

80ml (⅓ cup) water

FOR THE SPUDS:

500g (1lb 2oz) baby potatoes

2 tbsp rapeseed oil

1 tsp smoked paprika

sea salt and freshly ground black pepper

Put the potatoes in a large pot of salted water. Bring to a boil, then reduce the heat and simmer for 15-20 minutes, until the potatoes are tender all the way through. Drain the potatoes and let them cool slightly.

Preheat your oven to 200°C (400°F).

Put the boiled potatoes on a baking tray. Use a fork, cup or potato masher (even your hand if the spuds are cool enough) to gently flatten each potato until they are 2.5cm (1in) thick. Drizzle the oil over the flattened potatoes. Season the tops and bottoms with the smoked paprika, salt and pepper.

Roast the potatoes in the preheated oven for 30-35 minutes, turning them over halfway through, until they are crispy and golden brown on both sides.

Meanwhile, to make the chilli beans, heat the oil in a saucepan on a medium heat. Add the onion and cook for 2-3 minutes, until it's starting to soften. Stir in the garlic, chilli and spices and cook for another 2 minutes.

Add the beans, passata and water. Stir to combine, then reduce the heat to low and simmer for 20-25 minutes, allowing the sauce to thicken. Season with salt and pepper to taste.

To serve, arrange the crispy smashed spuds on a serving plate, then spoon over the chilli beans. Scatter over a handful of grated Cheddar (if using), then add a few big spoonfuls of Greek yogurt and garnish with fresh coriander leaves.

TO SERVE:
a handful of grated Cheddar cheese (optional)
Greek yogurt
fresh coriander leaves

make it a meal
Double the quantities to make this into a midweek family meal. This is also gorgeous with a fried or poached egg.

A good burrata speaks for itself, but this dish is a perfect contrast of creamy and crispy, rich and punchy. It all comes together into a umami flavour bomb perfect for sharing, spooned over toasted sourdough or served with other small plates for a gathering.

burrata
with chilli, garlic, lentil & caper oil
SERVES 2

3 tbsp olive oil

2 garlic cloves, thinly sliced

6 tbsp cooked lentils, drained well and patted dry

1 tbsp capers, drained and rinsed

½ tsp chilli flakes

½ tsp smoked paprika

½ tsp lemon zest

¼ tsp sea salt

¼ tsp freshly ground black pepper

1 large burrata

TO GARNISH:

chopped fresh parsley

a pinch of flaky sea salt

TO SERVE:

toasted sourdough or flatbread

Heat the oil in a small frying pan on a medium-low heat. Add the garlic and cook for 1–2 minutes, until lightly golden and fragrant. Stir in the lentils and capers and cook for another 2 minutes, until crispy. Add the chilli flakes, smoked paprika, lemon zest and the salt and pepper. Stir for 30 seconds, then take the pan off the heat and let all those flavours infuse together for a few minutes.

Put the burrata on a serving plate. Spoon the crispy chilli, garlic, lentil and caper oil over the burrata, then garnish with chopped fresh parsley and a pinch of flaky sea salt. Serve immediately with toasted sourdough or flatbread.

Slow cooked in oil with garlic, rosemary and thyme, these confit butter beans soak up all the flavour. Perfect as a side dish, as a topping for toast or as the base of a nourishing brunch bowl, this little recipe showcases the butter bean in all its glory. I don't have a favourite bean, but these are my go-to when I'm introducing beans to others' diets.

confit butter beans
with garlic, rosemary & thyme
SERVES 4 AS A SIDE

500g (3 cups) cooked butter beans or 2 x 400g (14oz) tins, drained and rinsed

4 garlic cloves, smashed

2 sprigs of fresh rosemary

2 sprigs of fresh thyme

200ml (¾ cup + 4 tsp) olive oil

½ tsp smoked paprika (optional)

1 tsp sea salt

½ tsp cracked black pepper

zest of ½ lemon (optional)

TO SERVE:

crusty bread

Preheat the oven to 180°C (350°F).

Combine the butter beans, garlic, rosemary, thyme, oil, smoked paprika (if using), salt and pepper in a small baking dish. Press a piece of parchment paper directly on top of the beans, then transfer the dish to the preheated oven and cook for 30 minutes, stirring halfway through.

Remove the parchment paper, then cook for another 10–15 minutes, until the beans are golden and slightly crispy on the edges. Discard the rosemary and thyme stalks.

Allow the beans to cool slightly, then sprinkle with lemon zest (if using) just before serving. These beans are great with crusty bread.

This dish brings together crisp, fresh green beans with the warming flavours of spiced red onions and a tangy aubergine pickle. It's a great salad for barbecues and sharing plates.

green bean salad
with red onion & aubergine pickle
SERVES 4

- 2 tbsp olive oil
- 1 small red onion, thinly sliced
- 1 garlic clove, finely chopped
- ½ tsp ground cumin
- ½ tsp ground coriander
- ½ tsp smoked paprika
- ½ tsp Dijon mustard
- sea salt and freshly ground black pepper
- 300g (11oz) green beans, topped and tailed
- 2–3 tbsp aubergine pickle (page 17)

Heat 1 tablespoon of the oil in a frying pan on a medium heat. Add the red onion and cook for 5 minutes, stirring occasionally, until soft. Add the garlic, spices and mustard, then cook for another 2–3 minutes. Season with salt and pepper, then take the pan off the heat.

Bring a pot of salted water to a boil. Blanch the green beans for 2–3 minutes, then drain and rinse under cold running water to keep them bright green and crisp. Toss with the remaining tablespoon of oil and a pinch of salt.

To serve, pile up the green beans on a serving platter, then spoon over the warm red onion and the aubergine pickle.

Green bean salad with red onion and aubergine pickle

make it a meal
Add some crumbled feta and/or jammy soft-boiled eggs.

Burrata with chilli, garlic, lentil and caper oil

Confit butter beans with garlic, rosemary and thyme

pulse-powered changemakers

Behind every bubbling pot of black-eyed beans or perfectly roasted chickpeas is someone stirring the pot in a bigger way. Here are a few pulse pioneers worth shouting about.

BEANS IS HOW

Behind the cheeky phrasing is a serious goal: to double global bean consumption by 2028. Created by the SDG2 Advocacy Hub, the Beans Is How campaign brings chefs, growers and policy nerds together to solve problems from climate change to child nutrition with pulses. I'm chuffed to be a bean champion, waving the legume flag with them at every opportunity.

BLUE ZONES

This health and longevity movement, inspired by regions where people live the longest, constantly points to beans as the single most important food for longevity. Their books, meal plans and community programmes put pulses front and centre, especially in schools and workplaces.

BOLD BEAN CO.

Amelia Christie-Miller and her team are on a mission to seduce your palate, one jar of beans at a time. These aren't your sad, shrink-wrapped supermarket mush bombs – they're silky, flavour-packed legumes that deserve to be the star of the show. Their motto says it all: Better Beans = Better Meals.

BOSH!

The plant-based pin-ups of YouTube, BOSH! have done for beans what boy bands did for hair gel – they've made them cool, accessible and universally loved. From smoky stews and bowl food to family favourites, all with a healthy hit of pulses, millions of views can't be wrong.

HODMEDOD'S

If beans had an underground indie label, Hodmedod's would be it. They've been growing forgotten British pulses since before it was cool. From fava beans to Carlin peas, they've quietly rebooted the UK pulse scene with integrity, soil wisdom and zero fuss. There's nothing fancy about them – just proper crops and brilliant farmers – but they are the quiet radicals of regenerative agriculture.

POLLY BALDWIN

Fire-wielding gut-health guru Polly Baldwin has turned her Jolly Allotment into a bean-packed sanctuary for mind, body and soil. With her Jolly Trolley food truck, she serves seasonal, gluten-free dishes brimming with beans, veggies and flavour, all designed to heal and nourish with a wink back at you.

RIVERFORD

Veg box legends and bean believers Riverford don't just sneak pulses into recipes, they celebrate them. Whether it's borlotti beans in a summer salad or a warming winter dal, they keep pulses pulsing through the seasons, proving that a good recipe starts with what's growing, not what's flown in from Peru.

USA DRY PEA & LENTIL COUNCIL (USADPLC)

This organisation is the powerhouse behind US-grown pulses. Based in Idaho, they represent American pea, lentil and chickpea farmers, promoting pulses globally for trade, nutrition and sustainability. They're champions of climate-smart agriculture, pushing beans as both a market crop and a planetary solution.

The more I worked with beans, the more they revealed themselves as reliable, sustainable and full of possibility. They became more than an ingredient – they became the backbone of a better way to eat.

If salads had a flavour spectrum, this one would sit firmly at the smack-you-in-the-mouth end. Yes, it's got vegetables – earthy, roasted beets in all their jewel-toned glory – but this is no sad pile of leaves pretending to be dinner. The beets, roasted until they're sticky and intense, get a creamy counterfoil from the ricotta. But the real winner is the peas. Dressed in a minty, lemon-spiked concoction that wakes everything up, they add freshness, crunch and sweetness. Pile it up, spoon it on or eat it straight from the plate.

roast beetroot salad
with minty peas, pickled stems, beet leaves & ricotta
SERVES 4

4 medium beetroots (about 500g (1lb 2oz)), with stems and leaves attached

2–3 garlic cloves, left whole and unpeeled

2 tbsp olive oil

½ tsp sea salt

¼ tsp ground black pepper

FOR THE PICKLED STEMS:

80ml (⅓ cup) water

60ml (¼ cup) apple cider vinegar

1 tbsp golden caster sugar

1 tsp mustard seeds

½ tsp salt

Preheat the oven to 200°C (400°F).

Trim off the beetroot stems and cut them into pieces 2.5cm (1in) long for pickling. Save the leaves for the salad.

Tear off a large sheet of foil and put it on a baking tray. Put the whole, unpeeled beets and the garlic cloves on top, then drizzle with the oil and season with the salt and pepper. Wrap them up in the foil, making sure all the edges are tightly sealed. Put the tray in the preheated oven and roast for 45–60 minutes, until the beets are tender all the way through.

Carefully open the foil parcel (watch out for the steam that escapes). When the beets are cool enough to handle, peel them (keep the skins for a beetroot hummus – see the tip) and cut into wedges. Set the roasted garlic cloves aside to use with the peas.

Meanwhile, to pickle the stems, heat the water, vinegar, sugar, mustard seeds and salt in a small saucepan until warm. Put the beetroot stems in a clean jar or a heatproof bowl, then pour over the warm brine. Set aside to pickle for at least 30 minutes.

To make the minty peas, blanch the peas in a saucepan of boiling water for 2 minutes, then drain and rinse under cold

FOR THE MINTY PEAS:

200g (1½ cups) fresh or frozen peas

zest and juice of ½ lemon

2 tbsp chopped fresh mint

1 tbsp olive oil

½ tsp sea salt

TO FINISH:

100g (½ cup) ricotta cheese

2 tbsp pumpkin or sunflower seeds, toasted

running water to stop them from cooking further. Transfer to a bowl and toss with the lemon zest and juice, chopped fresh mint, oil and salt.

Squeeze the roasted garlic cloves out of their skins, then mash them to a purée with a fork and stir it into the minty peas.

To assemble, roughly tear the reserved beet leaves onto a large serving platter. Scatter over the roasted beetroot wedges and pickled stems, then spoon over the minty peas, dollop the ricotta on top and sprinkle with the toasted seeds. Finish with salt and pepper to taste.

waste not, want not

❶ **LIKE THIS, LOVE THAT:** If you like this salad, you'll love the salt-baked beetroot and leaf salad with goat cheese and pickled beet stalks in *Blasta Books #7: Wasted* by Conor Spacey. And if you've got extra milk or milk that's a day or two past its best, use the recipe in *Wasted* to make your own ricotta.

❷ **REPURPOSE YOUR PODS:** If you're using fresh peas in their pods, keep the pods and use them to make the crispy salt and pepper pods on page 14 or the podka on page 64.

❸ **BEETROOT HUMMUS:** Those roasted beetroot skins are full of flavour, so here's a little Brucie bonus: turn them into a beetroot hummus. Just purée the skins and add them to the basic hummus recipe on page 11.

A big bowl of broth and noodles is one of my favourite things to eat when I'm feeling under the weather or it's just one of those days. Using frozen beans here means you can make this all year round, but you can also add any seasonal veggies you like. Tempeh, tofu, black beans and edamame are all good here if you want to swap out the broad beans and peas.

pea & broad bean broth
with noodles
SERVES 4

2 tbsp rapeseed oil

1 onion, finely chopped

2–3 garlic cloves, finely chopped

400g (14oz) assorted mushrooms (such as chestnut, shiitake and oyster), sliced

a thumb-sized piece of fresh ginger, peeled and finely chopped

1 tbsp miso (any kind you like)

1 tsp chilli flakes

800ml (3⅓ cups) water

4 tbsp soy sauce

1 tbsp rice wine vinegar

400g (14oz) fresh or frozen broad beans

200g (1½ cups) fresh or frozen peas

200g (7oz) ramen or thin egg noodles

TO SERVE:

150g (1 cup) bean sprouts (page 8)

fresh coriander leaves

chilli oil, chilli crisp or rayu

lime wedges

Heat the oil in a large saucepan on a medium heat. Add the onion and garlic and cook for about 5 minutes, until softened. Add the mushrooms and cook for another 5 minutes, until they release their juices and begin to brown. Stir in the ginger, miso and chilli flakes and cook for 1 minute.

Pour in the water, soy sauce and vinegar. Bring to a gentle simmer and cook for 10 minutes. Stir in the broad beans and peas and simmer for another 5 minutes, until tender. Add the noodles and simmer for about 5 minutes (or according to the packet instructions), until they are cooked.

Divide the noodles among four bowls. Ladle over the hot broth, making sure to get plenty of beans, peas and mushrooms in each bowl. Top each bowl with bean sprouts, coriander leaves and a spoonful of chilli oil, chilli crisp or rayu. Serve with lime wedges on the side for squeezing over.

There are few better foods than a ripe tomato at the height of tomato season. And on a hot summer day, there are few better ways to enjoy them than in a bowl of gazpacho. I make the crispy beans all the time as a topping for salads, soups and even granola (yes, really!). The herb stalk pesto is a way of never wasting a thing and is handy to have in the fridge for absolutely anything.

roast tomato gazpacho
with crispy beans & pesto

SERVES 4

1kg (2¼lb) vine-ripened tomatoes, kept whole and on the vine

1 medium onion, unpeeled and quartered

4 garlic cloves, left whole and unpeeled

a handful of fresh herbs, such as thyme or oregano

2 tbsp olive oil, plus extra to serve

1 tsp sea salt

500ml (2 cups + 4 tsp) water (or as needed)

freshly ground black pepper

FOR THE CRISPY BEANS:

1 tbsp olive oil

200g (1 cup) cooked beans (butter beans, cannellini, fava, haricots, Carlin peas or brown lentils all work well)

Preheat the oven to 200°C (400°F).

To make the gazpacho, put the whole tomatoes on the vine, the quartered onion, unpeeled garlic cloves and herbs on a baking tray. Drizzle with the oil and sprinkle with the salt, then roast in the preheated oven for 30–40 minutes, until the tomatoes are soft and slightly caramelised.

Remove and discard the onion skins, then pop the roasted onion into a blender. Squeeze the roasted garlic from its skins and add it to the blender along with the roasted tomatoes, herbs, water and any juices that have collected on the baking tray. Blend until smooth. It will be thick, so add more water if needed to get it to the consistency you want. Taste and adjust the seasoning with salt and pepper. Chill in the fridge for at least 1 hour.

Meanwhile, to make the crispy beans, heat the oil in a frying pan on a medium-high heat. Add the beans and cook for 5–7 minutes, until they are all crispy and golden. Sprinkle with salt and set aside. (Or you can cook them in an air fryer on high for 4–6 minutes with no oil.)

To make the pesto, put everything in a blender and blitz until combined but still with a bit of texture.

To serve, pour the soup into bowls. Top each one with crispy beans, then drizzle with the herb stalk pesto and an extra swirl of oil.

try this
Instead of serving this as a cold gazpacho, you could heat the soup and use it as a sauce for pasta or fish.

FOR THE HERB STALK PESTO:

20g (¾oz) fresh herb stalks (basil and/or parsley, though a few bits of rocket work too)

1 garlic clove (optional)

60ml (¼ cup) olive oil

juice of ½ lemon (or a little water)

1 tbsp toasted nuts or seeds (pumpkin or sunflower)

½ tsp sea salt

On a cold, stormy weekend, nothing beats a slow-cooked stew, and this little number is just the thing. I've called for cannellini and borlotti beans, but you can use whatever big, creamy beans you like. And as a nod to Keith Floyd, make sure you use a nice red wine so that you can have a glass while the stew cooks.

beany, shroomy stew
with dumplings
SERVES 4

2 tbsp olive oil
1 onion, finely chopped
1 carrot, finely chopped
2 celery sticks, thinly sliced
2 garlic cloves, chopped
200g (7oz) white mushrooms, sliced
200g (7oz) chestnut mushrooms, sliced
2 tbsp tomato purée
1 tbsp miso, Marmite or Worcestershire sauce
500g (3 cups) cooked cannellini beans or 2 x 400g (14oz) tins, drained and rinsed
250g (1½ cups) cooked borlotti beans or 1 x 400g (14oz) tin, drained and rinsed
1 bunch of fresh thyme, chopped
2 bay leaves (optional)
200ml (¾ cup + 4 tsp) red wine
200ml (¾ cup + 4 tsp) water
sea salt and freshly ground black pepper

Heat the oil in a heavy-based casserole or large saucepan on a medium heat. Add the onion, carrot, celery and garlic and cook for 5–7 minutes, until softened. Add the mushrooms and cook for 5 minutes, until they release their juices and start to brown. Stir in the tomato purée and the miso, Marmite or Worcestershire and cook for 1 minute, then add the beans, thyme and bay leaves (if using).

Pour in the wine and water, season generously with salt and pepper and bring to a gentle simmer. Lower the heat and let the stew cook, uncovered, for 30–35 minutes, until nicely reduced.

Preheat the oven to 200°C (400°F).

To make the dumplings, whisk the flour, baking powder and a pinch of salt in a large bowl. Add the butter, then rub it into the flour with your fingertips until it resembles breadcrumbs. Mix in the grated cheese with a butter knife.

Pour the milk into the dry ingredients, then stir with the butter knife to form a dough. Turn out onto your clean worktop, then shape into a log and cut into eight pieces.

Remove the bay leaves from the stew. If you've used a casserole, arrange the dumplings on top. Otherwise, transfer the stew to a large baking dish, then arrange the dumplings on top. Bake, uncovered, in the preheated oven for 20–25 minutes, until the dumplings are golden and cooked through.

To serve, divide the stew and dumplings among four bowls. Top each one with a little extra grated cheese and parsley.

FOR THE DUMPLINGS:

200g (scant 1¾ cups) self-raising flour

1 tsp baking powder

30g (2 tbsp) butter, diced

75g (¾ cup) grated cheese (use up any odds and ends here, such as Cheddar, Parmesan or Pecorino), plus extra to serve

a handful of fresh parsley, leaves finely chopped, plus extra to garnish

120ml (½ cup) milk

This is the kind of meal that is so full of textures and rich flavours, you don't even realise it's meat free. My daughter is half-Italian, so we call these polpette when we make them. It's a versatile mixture that can also be made into veggie 'sausage' rolls, meatballs and burgers, and it can be made and shaped into the rissoles a day or two in advance.

lentil, walnut & mushroom rissoles

SERVES 4

- 20g (¾oz) dried mushrooms
- 1 tbsp olive oil, plus extra for cooking
- 1 onion, finely chopped
- 300g (1½ cups) assorted mushrooms (such as chestnut, shiitake and oyster), chopped
- 2 garlic cloves, finely chopped
- 2 tbsp chopped fresh flat-leaf parsley
- 2 tsp chopped fresh thyme
- 250g (1½ cups) cooked green lentils or 1 x 400g (14oz) tin, drained and rinsed
- 75g (¾ cup) grated Parmesan cheese, plus extra to serve
- 30g (⅓ cup) finely chopped walnuts
- 1 tsp Dijon mustard
- sea salt and freshly ground black pepper
- 3 tbsp plain flour

Put the dried mushrooms in a small bowl, cover with just-boiled water from the kettle and soak for 10–15 minutes. Strain and chop the mushrooms, reserving the liquid for the tomato sauce.

Heat the oil in a large frying pan on a medium heat. Add the onion and cook for 5 minutes, until softened. Add the fresh mushrooms and cook for 5–10 minutes, until they release their juices and begin to brown. Add the garlic and fresh herbs and cook for 3 minutes, then tip into a mixing bowl.

Add the chopped rehydrated mushrooms, lentils, cheese, walnuts and mustard, then season well with salt and pepper and stir to combine. Put half of the mixture in a food processor and whizz to a purée. Transfer the purée back into the bowl, then combine with the rest of the mixture and the flour. Shape into eight to 10 large rissoles, put them on a plate and chill in the fridge for 30 minutes.

Meanwhile, to make the sauce, heat the oil in a saucepan on a medium heat. Add the garlic and cook, stirring, for 1–2 minutes, just until the garlic turns golden. Use a slotted spoon to transfer the garlic to a small plate and set it aside.

Add the passata and the reserved mushroom soaking liquid to the oil left in the pan. Season with salt and pepper, then lower the heat and cook until it has reduced to a thick, unctuous sauce.

Preheat the oven to 200°C (400°F).

FOR THE TOMATO SAUCE:
2 tbsp olive oil
1 garlic clove, thinly sliced
500ml (2 cups + 4 tsp) passata

TO SERVE:
fresh basil or pesto (page 32)
warm crusty bread

Heat a splash of oil in a large non-stick frying pan on a medium heat. Working in batches so that you don't overcrowd the pan, add the rissoles and cook for 2–3 minutes on each side to give them a nice sear all over. Transfer to a baking tray and cook in the preheated oven for 10 minutes, until cooked through.

To serve, put the rissoles in a serving dish and pour over the sauce. Top with grated Parmesan, scatter with torn fresh basil or drizzle with pesto, and serve with warm crusty bread.

Cooking with care, cooking creatively

cooking sustainably are all one and the same.

5 ways with beans

Got some cooked or tinned beans and looking for inspiration for quick and easy ways to use them? Look no further. Beans bulk things up fast, add fibre and protein, and work brilliantly with spice.

1 SMASH FOR TOAST OR TACOS Smash warm beans with rapeseed oil, a squeeze of lemon, a little grated garlic, some chopped fresh herbs and a pinch of chilli flakes. Spread on sourdough toast or tuck them into a taco, topped with greens, for a 5-minute meal.

2 ADD HARISSA OR PESTO Stir a spoonful of harissa, pesto or any other punchy sauce through warm beans. Pile onto flatbread or add to a grain bowl.

3 WARM WITH GARLIC AND HERBS Gently heat cooked beans in olive oil with sliced garlic, a sprig of fresh thyme or rosemary and a pinch of flaky sea salt and pepper. Finish with a little lemon zest, then spread on toast.

4 ADD TO EGGS Toss cooked beans into scrambled eggs or add them to a frittata or shakshuka.

5 CRISP THEM UP Toss cooked beans with olive oil, salt, pepper and spices like smoked paprika or cumin. Roast them on a baking tray in an oven preheated to 200°C (400°F) or fry them in a non-stick pan on a high heat until golden and crunchy. Eat as is or scatter over anything for added crunch.

clearing the air: the truth about toots

Beans have long suffered the unfortunate fate of being the butt (pun entirely intended) of every fart joke going. But the truth is that farting is not only normal, it's a sign that your gut is doing its job. Beans feed your microbiome, stabilise blood sugar, lower cholesterol and even reduce the risk of diseases such as heart disease and type 2 diabetes. And yes, beans can also cause gas. The reason you might be feeling a bit bubbly is because beans are packed with fibre and prebiotics, the very things your gut microbiome loves most.

You see, when those complex carbs hit your large intestine, your friendly gut bacteria get to work fermenting fibre, and, well, releasing gas is just part of the job. In other words, a toot or two means your gut's in good shape. Honestly, if a little gas is the price of admission, I'd say that's a small price to pay for lifelong health. Bloating, on the other hand, isn't quite as welcome. That distended, sluggish feeling isn't the same as a healthy post-bean breeze. But there are ways to eat beans and avoid the bloat. Here are my top tips.

❶ **START SLOW** If your gut isn't used to beans, gradually ease them into your diet. Your microbiome needs time to catch up. Bean Queen status takes a while!

❷ **EAT FERMENTED OR SPROUTED BEANS** These are easier on the gut and still pack in all the nutrition. The sprouted beans recipe on page 8 is a good place to start.

❸ **RINSE YOUR BEANS** If you're using dried beans, soak them properly (ideally overnight – see page 5) and rinse them well. This helps to remove some of the oligosaccharides, i.e. the complex sugars responsible for gas.

❹ **COOK THEM THOROUGHLY** Undercooked beans can be hard to digest, so make sure they're tender and creamy by following the instructions on page 6.

❺ **HAVE A LAUGH** Let's be honest, farts can be funny. A bit of gas might raise an eyebrow, but in the right company, it'll get a laugh too. A healthy gut is worth a few giggles. Let it rip! (Preferably in a well-ventilated room.)

Leftover risotto rarely gets the second act it deserves. Enter these crispy little golden wonders, the less fussy cousin of arancini. They're crunchy on the outside, creamy within, and just so happen to fly the flag for zero-waste brilliance. Bright pops of sweet pea meet a zippy mint dressing that wakes the palate up with a slap and a wink, while the silky aquafaba mayo adds a plant-based swagger that dairy could only dream of. Serve them as small plates or canapés, or just stand at the kitchen counter eating them straight from the pan with a fork and no shame.

crispy pea risotto cakes
with mint dressing & aquafaba mayo
MAKES 12

2 tbsp olive oil

a knob of butter

1 small onion, finely chopped

2 garlic cloves, finely chopped

sea salt and freshly ground black pepper

200g (1 heaped cup) Arborio rice

a splash of white wine (optional)

400ml (1 ⅔ cups) hot vegetable stock

200g (1½ cups) frozen peas, thawed

75g (¾ cup) grated Parmesan cheese

50g (½ cup) fresh or dried breadcrumbs

2 eggs, lightly beaten

60ml (¼ cup) vegetable oil, for frying

If you don't have any leftover risotto (you need about 500g (2 cups) cooked risotto) and are making these from scratch, heat the olive oil and butter in a heavy-based casserole or saucepan on a medium heat. When the butter has melted, add the onion, garlic and a good pinch of salt and pepper. Cook gently for 6–8 minutes, until the onion has softened but not coloured.

Add the rice, then turn up the heat and cook, stirring, for 1 minute. Add the wine (if using) and let it bubble up and get absorbed into the rice before adding one ladleful of hot stock. Turn the heat down to a simmer and stir until the stock has been absorbed. Keep adding one ladleful of stock at a time, allowing each one to be absorbed before adding the next. Carry on adding the stock until the rice is soft but still with a slight bite. Check the seasoning, then remove the pan from the heat and allow to cool completely.

To make the cakes, put the cooled (or leftover) risotto in a large bowl with the thawed peas, grated Parmesan, breadcrumbs and eggs. Season with salt and pepper to taste, then mix everything together until well combined.

Divide the risotto mixture into 12 even portions, then roll each one into a ball and flatten it slightly into a cake. Put on a baking tray lined with non-stick baking paper and chill in the fridge for at least 2 hours, or until needed.

FOR THE MINT DRESSING:

a handful of fresh mint leaves, finely chopped
2 tbsp apple cider vinegar
1 tbsp caster sugar
3 tbsp hot water

TO SERVE:

aquafaba mayo (page 47)

To make the mint dressing, put the mint, vinegar and sugar in a small heatproof bowl, then pour over the hot water, stirring to dissolve the sugar and infuse the mint flavour into the vinegar. Check the seasoning, then set aside for 15–20 minutes to let the flavours marry together.

Heat the vegetable oil in a large frying pan on a medium-high heat. Working in batches so that you don't overcrowd the pan, add the risotto cakes and fry for 3–4 minutes on each side, until golden brown, crispy and heated through.

To serve, swipe some aquafaba mayo onto a plate. Add the crispy risotto cakes on top, then spoon over some mint dressing.

Burgers are a great way to introduce beans to even the most die-hard carnivores, and this burger means business. It's got structure, it's got bite, and thanks to the mighty Carlin pea, it's got serious flavour. None of that bland, beige nonsense here. And because a good burger is only as strong as its supporting cast, I've gone full beans ahead with bean ketchup and aquafaba mayo. Get ready to rethink everything you thought you knew about bean burgers.

the Bean Queen burger

MAKES 4

200g (1 cup) dried Carlin peas or 400g (2¼ cups) cooked
1 tbsp olive oil
1 small onion, finely chopped
1 carrot, grated
150g (5¼oz) chestnut mushrooms, finely chopped
2 garlic cloves, crushed
1 tsp chopped fresh thyme
1 tsp ground cumin
1 tsp smoked paprika
1 tsp ground coriander
½ tsp salt
¼ tsp freshly ground black pepper
50g (½ cup) fresh or dried breadcrumbs
1 tbsp tomato purée
1 tbsp miso, soy sauce, tamari, Marmite or Worcestershire – whatever your umami vibe is
vegetable oil, for cooking

FOR THE BEANY BURGER SAUCE:
3–4 tbsp aquafaba mayo (page 47)
2–3 tbsp black-eyed bean ketchup (page 49)

If you're using dried Carlin peas, soak them in plenty of cold water overnight, then drain and boil in fresh water for 45–50 minutes, until tender. Drain well.

Put the cooked peas in a bowl, then lightly mash them with a fork or potato masher, leaving some texture.

Heat the olive oil in a frying pan on a medium heat. Add the onion, carrot, mushrooms and garlic and cook for 5 minutes, until soft. Add the fresh thyme, spices, salt and pepper and cook for 1 minute.

Transfer the cooked vegetables to the bowl with the mashed Carlin peas. Stir in the breadcrumbs, tomato purée and whatever umami flavour bomb you're using. Mix until well combined and it all holds together. Check the seasoning and adjust as needed.

Divide the mixture into four equal portions and shape them into patties. Put them on a plate and chill in the fridge for at least 20 minutes to firm up.

Meanwhile, to make the burger sauce, simply mix the aquafaba mayo and black-eyed bean ketchup together.

When you're ready to cook, heat a little vegetable oil in a large non-stick frying pan on a medium heat. Add the burgers and cook for 4–5 minutes on each side, until golden and heated through. To make these into cheeseburgers, add a slice of cheese on top of each patty, cover the pan with a lid and cook for 1 minute, until the cheese has started to melt.

carlin peas

Carlin peas (also known as black peas, grey peas, maple peas or black badgers) date back to the 12th century in the UK and have been brought back by the mighty work of Hodmedod's and the blessing of ready-to-eat jarred ones from Bold Bean Co. In Northern England, Carlin peas were traditionally eaten as parched peas (the cooked peas are simply doused with malt vinegar) for Bonfire Night. They also make a great substitute for chickpeas in any dish.

TO SERVE:

mature Cheddar cheese, thinly sliced (optional)

4 sourdough or brioche burger buns, toasted

shredded lettuce

thick tomato slices

quick pickled red onions and/or pickled cucumbers

Build your burger with your choice of toppings, but for the full Bean Queen, spread both sides of a toasted sourdough or brioche bun with burger sauce. Add a handful of shredded lettuce and one or two thick tomato sliced to the bottom half, then put a burger on top, pile on some pickled red onions and/or pickled cucumbers and sandwich together with the top half of the bun.

what in the world is ...

aquafaba?

Aquafaba is the magical bean liquid that you've probably been pouring down the drain.

Aquafaba (Latin for 'bean water') is the starchy liquid in a can of chickpeas or left behind when you cook pulses like white beans. This humble liquid has found superstar status in plant-based cooking for its egg-like powers.

Thanks to its unique combo of protein and starch, aquafaba can whip, bind, emulsify and foam, making it an ideal egg or dairy alternative. In fact, just 3 tablespoons of aquafaba equal one whole egg, making it a favourite in vegan baking, meringues, mousses and even cocktails. But where it really shines is in an egg-free mayo like the one on the next page. Blitz it with oil, mustard, vinegar and salt, and you've got creamy magic.

What's especially brilliant about aquafaba is that it turns waste into wonder. Instead of tossing that liquid from your tin of chickpeas or pot of beans, you're using a by-product that's already right there, meaning no extra cost, no extra ingredients and a lot less waste. It's a clever way to honour the whole ingredient and make your cooking more sustainable.

And you don't have to stick with chickpeas, either. The liquid from other mild-flavoured beans like butter beans, cannellini or haricot beans work beautifully too. Just strain it well and use it cold. If it seems too thin, simmer it to thicken it slightly. When it's got the consistency of egg white, it's aquafaba gold.

You can keep aquafaba in the fridge for up to seven days or freeze it in an ice cube tray, then store the frozen cubes in a freezerproof bag for up to four months.

Creamy, dreamy and totally egg-free, this little number turns aquafaba (aka chickpea juice) or any other white bean cooking liquid into a luscious spread that's perfect for slathering, dipping, dolloping or dressing up just about anything. The magic of aquafaba comes from the starches and proteins that leach into the cooking water or canning liquid. These allow it to emulsify with oil, just like egg yolk does in a traditional mayo. If using home-cooked beans, reduce the cooking liquid until it's the consistency of egg whites. It's a zero-waste win for your kitchen and the planet.

aquafaba mayo

MAKES ABOUT 300ML (1¼ CUPS)

240ml (1 cup) rapeseed oil

120ml (½ cup) aquafaba (the liquid from 1 x 400g (14oz) tin of chickpeas)

2–3 tbsp apple cider vinegar, depending on how tangy you like it

1 tsp Dijon mustard

½ tsp sea salt

Let all your ingredients come up to room temperature for best results.

Pop everything in a blender and blitz for 45–60 seconds. Or you can put the ingredients in a large measuring jug and use a hand blender, but keep the blender at the bottom of the jug and blitz for 10 seconds before moving it up. Don't worry if the mayo looks a little thin, it will thicken more when it's chilled.

Spoon the mayo into a clean jar and keep it in the fridge for up to two weeks.

This homemade ketchup sneaks in some bean goodness. It's great with whatever you fancy or to add to cottage pies and stews. It also makes an excellent burger sauce when mixed with aquafaba mayo (page 47).

black-eyed bean ketchup

MAKES 1 LITRE (4¼ CUPS)

2 tbsp olive oil

1 onion, finely chopped

1 red pepper, diced

2 garlic cloves, finely chopped

1 tsp ground cumin

1 tsp ground coriander

1 tsp paprika

500g (3 cups) cooked black-eyed beans or 2 x 400g (14oz) tins, rinsed and drained

1 x 400g (14oz) tin of chopped tomatoes or 400ml (14fl oz) passata

100g (½ cup) light brown sugar

200ml (¾ cup + 4 tsp) water (to start with)

100ml (⅓ cup + 4 tsp) apple cider vinegar

1 tsp Dijon mustard

1 tsp salt

½ tsp freshly ground black pepper

a little chilli or harissa (optional for extra kick)

Sterilise your jars and lids by cleaning them in hot soapy water, then put them upside-down on a baking tray and pop them in an oven preheated to 180°C (350°F) for at least 15 minutes or until you're ready to use them. Alternatively, run them through your dishwasher and leave them in there until you're ready.

Heat the oil in a large saucepan on a medium heat. Add the onion and cook for about 5 minutes, until softened. Add the red pepper, garlic and spices and cook for 3–4 minutes.

Stir in the beans, tomatoes, brown sugar, water, vinegar, mustard, salt, pepper and a little chilli or harissa (if using). Bring to a boil, then reduce the heat to low and simmer for 30–40 minutes, stirring occasionally, until thickened.

Take the pan off the heat and allow the mixture to cool slightly, then use a hand blender to purée until smooth. If it has reduced too much, add a little more water until you get a good pouring consistency. Taste the ketchup and adjust the seasoning, adding more salt or sugar if needed.

Pour the black-eyed bean ketchup into your sterilised jars or bottles, then let it cool to room temperature before sealing. Store in a cool, dry place. Once opened, keep in the fridge and use within one month.

Slather it on toast, drizzle it over porridge, spread it on cakes or dollop it on ice cream.

This silky, protein- and fibre-packed chocolate spread is a game-changer. It's a wholesome twist on shop-bought chocolate spreads, without the refined sugars or palm oil. It's rich, fudgy and perfectly sweet. Slather it on toast, drizzle it over porridge, spread it on cakes or dollop it on ice cream.

chocolate bean spread

MAKES APPROX. 360ML (1½ CUPS)

150g (5¼oz) Medjool dates, pitted

250g (1½ cups) cooked creamy beans or 1 x 400g (14oz) tin, drained and rinsed (try black beans, butter beans, cannellini beans, chickpeas or haricot beans)

45g (heaped ⅓ cup) good-quality cocoa powder

2 tbsp flaxseeds (or ground flaxseeds for a smoother texture)

1 tsp vanilla extract

¼ tsp sea salt

1 tbsp maple syrup (optional)

Sterilise a jar and its lid by cleaning them in hot soapy water, then putting them upside-down on a baking tray and popping them in an oven preheated to 180°C (350°F) for at least 15 minutes or until you're ready to use them. Alternatively, run them through your dishwasher and leave them in there until you're ready.

Soak the pitted dates in warm water for 5–10 minutes to soften. Drain but keep the soaking water.

Put the dates in a food processor or high-speed blender with the beans, cocoa powder, flaxseeds, vanilla and salt. Blitz to combine. With the motor running, gradually add 60–80ml (¼–⅓ cup) of the reserved soaking water, blending until it's smooth and creamy. Scrape down the sides of the blender or food processor as needed. Adjust the sweetness (add a few more dates or the optional maple syrup) or the richness (add more cocoa) to taste, then
blend again.

Transfer the spread to the sterilised jar, seal with a lid and store in the fridge for up to five days.

A basic muffin mix is a great recipe to have in your repertoire. The berries add an antioxidant and vitamin boost, while the beans and yogurt add protein and fibre – not bad for a little sweet morning treat with your cuppa. Plus you can vary the flavour profile – try adding chocolate chips, chopped nuts, diced apple or pear, or a little spice like cinnamon or ginger. I have also made these with pumpkin, carrots and beetroot jam for a veggie boost. Frozen berries work well here all year round, but these muffins are a great way to use fresh, in-season berries that are past their best.

berry bean muffins

MAKES 12

250g (1¼ cups) cooked white beans (I use cannellini) or 1 x 400g (14oz) tin, drained and rinsed

3 large eggs

1 tsp vanilla extract

200g (scant 1¾ cups) self-raising flour

100g (½ cup) golden caster sugar

1 tsp baking powder

½ tsp baking soda

¼ tsp salt

120g (½ cup) Greek yogurt

60g (4 tbsp) unsalted butter, melted

zest of ½ lemon (optional)

200g (1¼ cups) fresh or frozen berries, such as blueberries, raspberries and blackberries

2 tbsp jam or curd (optional)

Preheat your oven to 180°C (350°F). Line a muffin tin with paper liners or grease the muffin cups with cooking spray.

Put the beans, eggs and vanilla in a food processor. Blend to a smooth, thick paste.

Put the flour, sugar, baking powder, baking soda and salt in a large bowl and whisk to combine.

In another bowl, mix the yogurt, melted butter and lemon zest (if using). Add the bean purée and mix until combined.

Gradually add the wet ingredients to the dry ingredients, mixing until you have a smooth batter, then gently fold in the berries.

Spoon the batter into the prepared muffin cups, filling each one about two-thirds full. If using jam or curd, add a spoonful of the muffin batter to each prepared cup, then add ½ teaspoon of jam or curd, then top with more batter.

Bake in the preheated oven for 22–25 minutes, until a skewer inserted into the centre of a muffin comes out clean or with just a few crumbs clinging to it.

Allow the muffins to cool in the tin for a few minutes before transferring them to a wire rack to cool completely.

I came up with this recipe a few years ago when I wanted to do some festive baking with beans at Christmastime. The idea for a spiced crinkle cookie stuck in my head, and these are the result. They're a crowd-pleaser at any time of year, but Santa gave them a big thumbs-up.

chocolate chip, ginger & white bean crinkle cookies

MAKES APPROX. 20

150g (¾ cup) cooked white beans (I use cannellini)

150g (¾ cup) light brown sugar

110g (½ cup) unsalted butter, softened

1 large egg

1 tsp vanilla extract

240g (2 cups) plain flour (you can use buckwheat, spelt or other alternatives too)

2 tsp ground ginger

1 tsp ground cinnamon

½ tsp ground nutmeg

1 tsp baking soda

¼ tsp salt

100g (½ cup) dark chocolate chips

50g (⅓ cup) finely chopped crystallised ginger

60g (½ cup) icing sugar, for rolling

Blend the beans, sugar, butter, egg and vanilla in a food processor.

Put the flour, spices, baking soda and salt in a large bowl and mix to combine. Add the bean purée and fold it through, but don't overmix. Stir in the chocolate chips and the crystallised ginger.

Cover the bowl with cling film and chill the dough in the fridge for at least 30 minutes to make it easier to handle.

Preheat your oven to 180°C (350°F). Line two baking trays with non-stick baking paper.

Put the icing sugar in a small bowl. Scoop out tablespoon-sized portions of cookie dough and roll them into balls. Roll each ball in icing sugar until fully coated.

Put the coated balls on the lined trays, leaving space between each one to give them room to spread. Press each one down slightly.

Bake in the preheated oven for 18–20 minutes, until the edges are set and the tops have cracked. These cookies are crunchy on the outside with a spongy centre, but if you would like an even crunchier cookie, cook them for a few minutes longer.

Allow the cookies to cool on the trays for a few minutes before transferring them to a wire rack to cool completely. They will keep in an airtight container for up to three days.

Years ago, I drew the crowds to one of my eateries with fresh doughnuts, made with slowly fermented dough, homemade custard and creative fillings. It was a true labour of love, but it's also how I met the love of my life. He came for the doughnuts but fell for the cook (or maybe he fancied the cook and fell for the doughnuts?). Either way, he never stops asking for them.

dreamy beany doughnuts

MAKES 15

FOR THE DOUGH:

150ml (½ cup + 2 tbsp) water

500g (4¼ cups) strong white flour

60g (heaped ¼ cup) golden caster sugar

4 eggs

1 x 7g sachet (1½ tsp) fast-action dried yeast

2 tsp fine sea salt

125g (½ cup + 1 tbsp) unsalted butter, diced and softened

FOR THE BEAN CUSTARD:

125g (¾ cup) cooked white beans

4 egg yolks

60g (heaped ¼ cup) caster sugar

1½ tbsp cornflour

1 tbsp plain flour

350ml (1½ cups) full-fat milk

1 vanilla bean, split in half lengthways and seeds scraped out, or 1 tsp vanilla bean paste

icing sugar, for dusting

200ml (¾ cup + 4 tsp) cream

To make the dough, pour the water into the bowl of a stand mixer fitted with a dough hook, then add all the dough ingredients except the butter. Mix on a medium speed for 8 minutes, until the dough forms a ball and pulls away from the sides of the bowl. Let the dough rest for 1 minute.

Add the softened butter 30g (2 tablespoons) at a time, allowing it to fully mix in on a medium speed before adding more. Once all the butter has been incorporated, mix on a high speed for 5 minutes, until the dough is glossy, smooth and elastic. Cover the bowl with a clean tea towel and leave to prove in a warm, draught-free place for about 2 hours, until doubled in size.

Knock the dough back briefly, cover it again, then put it in the fridge overnight.

Now make your custard base for the next day. Put the cooked beans in a blender or food processor and blitz to a smooth purée.

In a large mixing bowl, whisk together the egg yolks and sugar until they turn pale and slightly thickened, then whisk in the cornflour and plain flour.

Put the milk and vanilla in a heavy-based saucepan. Bring to a gentle simmer on a medium heat, whisking frequently. Remove the pan from the heat and let it cool for 1 minute. Remove the vanilla bean.

Slowly add the hot milk to the egg mixture, whisking all the time to prevent the eggs from scrambling, then return the

mixture to the saucepan. Stir in the bean purée. Whisking continuously, bring the mixture back to simmer, then cook for about 1 minute, until the custard thickens enough to coat the back of a spoon.

Pour the custard into a clean bowl through a fine mesh sieve. Dust the top with icing sugar to prevent a skin forming and allow to cool, then cover the bowl with cling film and refrigerate overnight.

The next day, line a baking tray with non-stick baking paper. Take the dough out of the fridge and cut it into 15 x 75g (2½oz) pieces. Roll each piece into a smooth, tight ball, then put them on the lined tray, leaving space between them. Cover loosely with a clean tea towel and leave to rise in a warm, draught-free place for 4 hours, until doubled in size.

Heat the sunflower oil in a deep-fryer to 180°C (350°F). If you don't have a deep-fryer fill a heavy-based, high-sided saucepan no more than halfway full of oil. Put the caster sugar in a bowl and set aside.

With the doughnuts still on the baking paper, cut around each one. Working in batches of only two or three doughnuts at a time, put them into the hot oil. The paper will come away easily after a few seconds, and the doughnuts will keep their shape perfectly.

Cook for 2½ minutes per side, until golden brown. Drain on a plate lined with kitchen paper. While still warm, toss the doughnuts in the caster sugar. Repeat with the remaining doughnuts, making sure you bring the oil back up to 180°C (350°F) before frying each batch. Too hot = burnt outside/raw inside; too low = greasy doughnuts.

Once cooled, make a small hole in each doughnut along the white line that will have naturally formed between the top and bottom.

Whip your cream to stiff peaks. In a separate bowl, whisk the custard until smooth, then fold in the whipped cream.

Fill a piping bag with the bean custard and pipe it into the hole in each doughnut. Eat immediately.

FOR FRYING & COATING:

sunflower oil

100g (½ cup) caster sugar

Another classic pud with a clever twist. It's rich, yet lighter than the usual dense pudding. And with the beans and parsnip in it, you can feel virtuous even as you drown it in toffee sauce.

sticky toffee bean & parsnip pudding

SERVES 6

150g (1 cup) pitted dates, chopped
180ml (¾ cup) boiling water
1 tsp baking soda
150g (¾ cup) cooked beans (any kind)
1 parsnip, grated
2 tbsp treacle
1 tsp vanilla extract
1 tsp ground cinnamon
½ tsp ground ginger
½ tsp sea salt
125g (¾ cup) dark brown sugar
90g (6 tbsp) unsalted butter, melted, plus extra for greasing
3 eggs
150g (1¼ cups) self-raising flour
1½ tsp baking powder

FOR THE TOFFEE SAUCE:

150g (¾ cup) dark brown sugar
75g (5 tbsp) unsalted butter
240ml (1 cup) cream
flaky sea salt

TO SERVE:

vanilla ice cream

Preheat the oven to 180°C (350°F). Grease a rectangular baking tin, baking dish or six ramekins with melted butter. If you're using a tin, line it with non-stick baking paper too.

Put the chopped dates in a bowl, pour over the boiling water and stir in the baking soda. Let it sit for 10 minutes to soften the dates.

Transfer the dates and their soaking liquid to a blender or food processor with the beans, parsnip, treacle, vanilla, cinnamon, ginger and salt. Blend until smooth.

Add the brown sugar, melted butter and eggs and pulse to combine. Add the flour and baking powder and blend until smooth.

Pour the batter into the tin or baking dish or divide it among the ramekins. Bake in the preheated oven for 30–40 minutes if using a baking tin or dish or for 18–20 minutes if using ramekins, until cooked through and golden.

Meanwhile, to make the toffee sauce, put the sugar, butter and cream in a saucepan on a medium heat. Simmer for 3–5 minutes, stirring constantly, until thickened, then stir in a pinch of flaky sea salt.

To serve, cut the sticky toffee pudding into slices and spoon it into a bowl or serve it straight from the ramekins. Add one or two scoops of ice cream, then pour over a pool of sauce. It's worth the calories.

This classic crème brûlée with a surprising beany twist is luxuriously smooth and subtly sweet, with the added bonus of the protein and fibre that the beans provide, making this a delicious, nutritious indulgence that will impress even the biggest bean sceptics.

white bean crème brûlée

SERVES 6

250g (1½ cups) cooked white beans or 1 x 400g (14oz) tin, drained and rinsed

500ml (2 cups + 4 tsp) full-fat milk

100g (½ cup) golden caster sugar

1 vanilla bean, split in half lengthways and seeds scraped out, or 2 tsp vanilla extract

4 large egg yolks

6 tbsp light or dark brown sugar, for caramelising the tops

Preheat your oven to 160°C (325°F).

Put the beans and milk in a blender and blitz until completely smooth. Transfer to a saucepan with the sugar and vanilla and cook, stirring gently, on a medium heat just until the mixture starts to simmer – don't let it boil. Remove the pan from the heat.

In a large bowl, whisk the egg yolks until smooth. Slowly pour a small amount of the warm milk mixture into the egg yolks while whisking constantly. Gradually add the rest of the milk, whisking continuously to prevent curdling. Remove the vanilla bean, if using. Pour the custard into a clean jug through a fine mesh sieve to remove any bean skins that didn't get completely blended.

Divide the custard evenly among six ramekins. Put the ramekins in a roasting tin or a deep baking dish, then fill the tin or dish with hot water until it comes halfway up the sides of the ramekins.

Transfer to the preheated oven and bake for 30–35 minutes, until the custard is just set but still slightly wobbly in the centre. Take the ramekins out of the tin or dish and allow to cool, then chill in the fridge for at least 3 hours (or overnight for best results).

Sprinkle 1 tablespoon of brown sugar in an even layer over the top of the chilled custard in each ramekin. Using a kitchen blowtorch, caramelise the sugar until it's golden and crisp. Alternatively, you can put the ramekins under a hot grill for 1–2 minutes. Let the caramelised tops cool for a minute until hardened, then serve immediately.

I created this celebratory centrepiece for a dinner I cooked at Fortnum & Mason in London, where I was showing how beans could feature in a fine dining experience. The pudding was my salute to a retro classic. And after all the effort you've gone to to make this, don't skip the fiery flambé at the end to make it a true showstopper.

black bean baked Alaska

SERVES 8–10

250g (1½ cups) cooked black beans or 1 x 400g (14oz) tin, drained and rinsed

100g (½ cup) caster sugar

3 large eggs

3 tbsp vegetable oil

1½ tsp vanilla extract

45g (4½ tbsp) unsweetened cocoa powder

1 tsp baking powder

a pinch of salt

1 jar of blackcurrant, blackberry or cherry jam

FOR THE MERINGUE:

6 large egg whites

350g (1¾ cups) caster sugar

2 tsp white wine vinegar

TO FINISH:

1 litre (4¼ cups) good-quality vanilla ice cream

a shot of brandy, to flambé (optional)

Soften the ice cream, then whip it up to make it smooth and spreadable. Line a freezerproof bowl that's slightly smaller than your 20cm (8in) cake tin with greaseproof paper or cling film, then pour the whipped ice cream into it and smooth the top. Put it back in the freezer to freeze again into a neat half-moon mound.

Preheat the oven to 170°C (340°F). Line a 20cm (8in) cake tin with non-stick baking paper.

Put the beans in a food processor with the sugar, eggs, oil and vanilla and blend to a smooth purée. Add the cocoa powder, baking powder and salt and blend just until fully combined.

Pour the batter into the lined cake tin and bake in the preheated oven for 15–18 minutes, until cooked through and a skewer inserted into the centre comes out clean. Cool on a wire rack.

To make the meringue, whisk the egg whites to stiff peaks in a spotlessly clean, dry bowl. Add the sugar 1 tablespoon at a time while whisking continuously until you have a thick, glossy mixture that holds its shape when the beaters are lifted away from the bowl. Quickly beat in the vinegar.

To assemble, take the ice cream out of the freezer and let it soften slightly so that you can unmould it from the bowl. Put the black bean cake on a serving platter, then spread it with a thick layer of jam. Put the ice cream mound in the middle of the cake, then spoon or pipe the meringue all over the top and sides in a nice thick layer. Use a kitchen blowtorch to give the meringue a golden char. For an extra-special finishing touch, drizzle over the brandy, then stand back, light it with a match or the blowtorch and let the flames die down. Cut into slices to serve.

waste not, want not
If you make the bean custard on page 54 or the crème brûlée on page 58, save the egg whites to use in the meringue here.

This rich, fudgy chocolate cake can be made as a celebration layer cake, a traybake or brownie-style. To pack in even more bean goodness, the chocolate bean spread on page 51 makes a great filling to sandwich the layer cakes together, which then get topped with the icing. You can also use the spread for topping the traybake. For brownies, just leave the traybake plain.

black bean mocha fudge cake

MAKES 1 X THREE-LAYER CAKE OR 1 X TRAYBAKE

500g (3 cups) cooked black beans or 2 x 400g (14oz) tins, drained and rinsed

250g (1¼ cups) caster sugar

6 large eggs

6 tbsp vegetable oil

1 tbsp vanilla extract

75g (½ cup + 1½ tbsp) unsweetened cocoa powder

2 tbsp used coffee grounds (optional)

1½ tsp baking powder

½ tsp salt

FOR THE ICING:*

30g (2 tbsp) butter, softened

3–4 tbsp icing sugar

1–2 tbsp cocoa powder

1 tsp vanilla extract

FOR THE LAYER CAKE FILLING:

1 batch of chocolate bean spread (page 51)

Double the quantities if making a traybake.

Preheat the oven to 180°C (350°F). To make a layer cake, grease 3 x 20cm (8in) cake tins and line with non-stick baking paper. To make a traybake, grease and line a 23cm x 33cm (9in x 13in) baking tin.

Put the beans in a food processor with the sugar, eggs, oil and vanilla and blend until smooth. Add the cocoa powder, coffee grounds (if using), baking powder and salt and blend just until fully combined.

Divide the batter among the three lined tins if making the layer cake or pour it all into the rectangular tin if making a traybake. Bake in the preheated oven for 10–12 minutes for the three layers or for 18–22 minutes for the traybake, until a skewer inserted into the centre comes out clean.

Allow the cake(s) to cool in the tin(s) for 10 minutes, then transfer to a wire rack to cool completely before icing.

To make the icing, beat together the butter, icing sugar, cocoa powder and vanilla until smooth. Adjust the consistency with a splash of just-boiled water from the kettle if needed to thin it down a bit to a spreadable icing consistency.

To make the three-layer cake, put one of the cakes on a serving platter, then spread half of the chocolate bean spread all over the top, going right to the edges. Put a second cake on top and cover with the rest of the spread. Finish with the final cake, then spread that with the icing. If making the traybake, simply spread the chocolate bean spread or the icing all over the top of the cake. Cut into slices or squares to serve.

We gave the humble bean pod its moment in the sun as a crispy, no-waste snack in the recipe for salt and pepper pods on page 14. It was proof that even the bits most people bin can be downright delicious. But pods, it turns out, have another party trick. Meet podka, an infusion that captures the green, grassy flavour of fresh bean or pea pods. It's just vodka (or gin if you're a juniper fan) steeped with the very thing you'd usually throw away. The result? A drink that tastes like the smell of a June garden: bright, clean and quietly surprising. This isn't a gimmick; it's genuinely good. Serve it straight from the freezer in a martini or mix it with tonic for a podka tonic and sip in satisfaction knowing that nothing went to waste.

podka

MAKES 700ML (24FL OZ)

2 generous handfuls of fresh broad bean or pea pods, thoroughly washed

1 x 700ml (24fl oz) bottle of vodka (or gin)

OPTIONAL FLAVOUR BOOSTERS:

lemon zest

a few fresh mint leaves

a pinch of fennel or coriander seeds

Sterilise a 1-litre (4¼-cup) jar and its lid by cleaning them in hot soapy water, then put them upside-down on a baking tray and pop them in an oven preheated to 180°C (350°F) for at least 15 minutes or until you're ready to use them. Alternatively, run them through your dishwasher and leave them in there until you're ready.

Snap the clean pods into small pieces to release more flavour. Put them in the sterilised jar and pour in the vodka or gin, making sure the pods are fully covered. Drop in any optional flavour boosters, if using.

Seal and store in a cool, dark place for three to five days, giving the jar a gentle shake every day. Taste it after three days. When the flavour is green, fresh and fragrant, strain the podka through a muslin, coffee filter or fine mesh sieve.

Transfer the podka to a clean 1-litre (4¼-cup) bottle and store in the fridge or freezer. The podka will keep for a few months, but it's best drunk within four to six weeks for maximum pod perfection.

Named after Kate, a certain fabulous journalist who has made 'lush' her signature, this one's for you, my lovely. I created it for a cookery demo where Kate held the mic and I wielded the shaker. I use rhubarb in this when it's in season, but blackberries, gooseberries or blackcurrants all play well too. Or you can cheat and use the dregs of a jar of jam rather than make your own syrup. As for measurements, this is all about balance, not precision. Trust your instincts, taste as you go and make it lush.

the faba-lush cocktail

MAKES 1

8–10 ice cubes

3 tbsp base spirit, such as gin, vodka or mezcal

2 tbsp aquafaba

1–2 tbsp lemon juice

prosecco to finish for a bit of fizz (optional)

FOR THE FRUIT SYRUP:

2–3 rhubarb stalks, chopped

4 tbsp caster sugar

4 tbsp water

1 small strip of lemon peel

Chill your martini glass with some of the ice cubes.

To make the fruit syrup, put the rhubarb, sugar, water and lemon peel in a small saucepan on a medium-high heat. Bring to a boil, stirring occasionally. Reduce the heat to low and simmer, still stirring occasionally, for 5–6 minutes, until the fruit breaks down. Strain the syrup into a bowl through a fine mesh sieve, pressing down on the solids in the sieve to extract as much flavour as possible. Keep what doesn't pass through the sieve and use it in a smoothie or put it on top of your granola. You can store the syrup in the fridge for up to a week or freeze it in an ice cube tray.

Pour 2 tablespoons of the fruit syrup into a cocktail shaker. Add your base spirit, aquafaba and 1 tablespoon of lemon juice and shake for 15–20 seconds. Taste it and add another tablespoon of lemon juice if you think it needs it. Add the ice from your martini glass and a few extra cubes and shake vigorously until the shaker gets cold.

Strain into the chilled martini glass. Top up with prosecco (if using) for a bit of fizz.

try this
To go all out and make candied rhubarb skins as a garnish, put 2 tablespoons of caster sugar in a small heatproof bowl, then pour in 1 tablespoon of just-boiled water from the kettle and whisk until the sugar has dissolved. Line a baking tray with non-stick baking paper. Use a peeler to cut a rhubarb stalk into thin ribbons, then brush them with this sugar glaze and leave to set.

Blasta Books

an imprint of Nine Bean Rows

23 Mountjoy Square

Dublin, D01 E0F8

Ireland

@blastabooks

blastabooks.com

First published 2026

Text copyright © Ali Honour, 2026

ISBN: 978-1-0684050-1-3

Editor: Kristin Jensen

Designer: Jane Matthews

Photographer: Jo Murphy

Food stylist: Charlotte O'Connell

Cover illustrator: Ella Ginn

Proofreader: Jocelyn Doyle

Printed by L&C Printing Group, Poland

This product is made of material from well-managed, FSC®-certified forests and other controlled sources.

All rights reserved.

No part of this publication may be copied, reproduced or transmitted in any form or by any means without written permission of the publishers.

A CIP catalogue record for this book is available from the British Library.

For EU product safety concerns, contact info@ninebeanrowsbooks.com.

10 9 8 7 6 5 4 3 2 1

about the author

Ali Honour is a creative force driving a better future through what we eat. She's a chef, food systems disruptor and outspoken advocate for sustainable eating, known for turning humble beans and vegetables into culinary and climate heroes. With three decades of experience across professional kitchens, food education and advocacy, Ali blends culinary creativity with deep-rooted purpose to prove that good food can – and must – be good for people and planet.

Trained as a chef and shaped by years working at the intersection of hospitality, food waste and sustainability, Ali is a natural entrepreneur who has run several successful businesses over the years. Ali now leads pioneering zero-waste catering for major events, reimagining menus through a climate-conscious lens, and supports farmers and producers championing regenerative crops. Ali's work spans grassroots initiatives and global platforms alike, including key role collaborations with the Chefs' Manifesto and the Beans Is How campaign, the Blue Earth Summit, Dairygold and EUFIC, among others.

A natural communicator and creative problem-solver, Ali brings warmth, wit and rigour to every plate and every project. From public demos to behind-the-scenes strategy, she inspires real change through practical, delicious solutions, leading a bold movement to inspire change. Ali invites us all to rethink what's on our plate and to embrace a future where food is fairer, cleaner, tastier and pulse-powered too.

@honouryourfood